# THE MAN YANG TREE

*a kind of holiness*

Anthea Dove

*for Daniel*

*with love always*

*& thanks for*

*the stunning foreword!*

*Anthea,*

**RB**

*Rossendale Books*

Front Cover image: Reinhild Raistrick

Published by Lulu Enterprises Inc.
3101 Hillsborough Street
Suite 210
Raleigh, NC 27607-5436
United States of America

Published in paperback 2015
Category: Christianity
Copyright Anthea Dove © 2015
ISBN : 978-1-326-16298-6

This book is dedicated to Jill Dalladay
with gratitude and affection,
and, as always, to Chris

# Contents

# Foreword

This collection of reflections is short, wise and spiritually rich. I needed space after each one to contemplate a little on the mystery of life it explored. The scenes are selected from all over the place – childhood, a concert, a peacock, prison cells, the cruelty of April, a valley of buttercups, blue moons . . . Many themes of Incarnation run through this book – the theme of noticing, of waiting, of recognising, of ever-renewing life, of final blossoming. Like the Man Yang Tree, one day, sooner or later, and perhaps at the most unexpected addresses, things finally flourish into their true being. And that is true for all of us.

There are nostalgic shadows of poignancy, even pathos as the reader is called into the land of memories, where what seemed ordinary enough when they first happened, but, in recollection, bring us to the verge of tears – of happiness and loss. The author's vividly-remembered childhood experiences surely play a part in her 'spontaneous joy' in the smallest epiphanies.

This collection is thankfully devoid of religiosity and shallow devotion. There is no superficial proselytising, preaching or piety about the writing. The reflections on the chosen experiences stay resolutely based on the hidden beauty of things, on the wonder of life, the deeper way of living. Readers are left free for their own spiritual interpretations. 'To thine own self be true' is the wise phrase that the author tries to live by, and write by, as she continues to explore the profoundest reality of things. And of this be sure – the author's sensitivity to the love and meaning at the heart of everything comes from a very holy place.

Among the gems in this book I particularly liked Red House (about change;16), Hospital (about love;21), Pebble (about contemplation;43), Court Case (about disappointment;51), Morning Glory (about hope;53), Widow (about loss;60), Remembering (about re-membering;61), Hankering (about purity;62), Coffee after Church (about noticing;70), Forgiveness (about another way;90), Other Worlds (about faith;91), The Great Loneliness (about a question;99), Swinging on a Star about the eternal child within;106).

Daniel O'Leary

# Introduction

*"Whatsoever things are true, whatsoever things are honest, whatsoever things are just, whatsoever things are pure, whatsoever things are lovely, whatsoever things are of good report; if there be any virtue, and if there be any praise, think on these things."*
**Philippians 4 v 8**

I suppose this book is more than anything about a kind of holiness, the holiness in beauty, in people and places and nature, the holiness of humanity. As I grow older I have time to reflect and to notice more intimately what is happening in the world around me. It seems to me that God moves not only in a mysterious way but also in hidden and surprising ways, so that holiness can be found in the actions of a declared atheist, in the remorse of a violent criminal, in puddles and waste land as well as in waterfalls and windflowers and the Man Yang Tree. In a desolate back street of a noisy city, we can look up to see the magic of a murmuration of starlings, and receive a sense of God.

## After-Thought

When I wrote this Introduction, I did indeed intend to 'think on these things" and write about them.

But events have overtaken me, and as horrendous happenings have been occurring in so many places in the world, I feel compelled to reflect and write about some of the things which are very far from being "lovely" or of "good report", but which touch all our lives.

# 1  THE MAN YANG TREE - 2012

Of the Man Yang tree you could say:
"It's a lesson in patience and hope"
or you could simply be overjoyed, and
overwhelmed by the beauty of its flowers.
This tree came from the forests of China
thirty years ago.
It stood in the garden, healthy but barren,
until today.
Today, in this dark summer of grumbles
and unrelenting rain, the Man Yang Tree is
in flower, exquisitely beautiful.

The original specimen of this tree was
introduced to cultivation in 1907 and
named in honour of the plant collector
Augustine Henry. In 2012, the Cambridge
Botanic Gardens decided to give the tree a
common name [in addition to the Latin
*Emmenopteryis henryi* ] and gave an open
invitation for people to choose this new
name. A twelve-year-old boy, the great,
great nephew of Augustine Henry,
suggested that it should be called after Man

Yang, the favourite Chinese plant collector of his great, great uncle. And so it was.

## 2 MILLGATE

Early in the morning, the garden is so quiet, enclosed like a nunnery, but unlike any nunnery I've known, exuberant, with trees and shrubs in abundant bloom. Somewhere below these walls the wide, wild Swale tumbles over a weir, so there is a constant sound of water underlying the quiet within the walls. I heard an insect, a bee, perhaps, humming already on its eager flight, and there are different birds singing, twittering and cooing. But for all these noises, the garden seems to hold silence, and it seems natural to be still. The scents after last night's rain are delicate in the air, and everywhere I walk down the narrow winding paths, blossom brushes against my body and my face. On the wall, in graceful lettering, these words are carved:

*We are a garden wall'd around,*
*chosen and made peculiar ground;*
*a little spot enclos'd by grace*
*out of the world's wide wilderness.*
*Isaac Watts 1674-1748*

Yet even here, in this paradise, my thoughts stray to that wilderness outside.

## 3  DEATH ROW

When I was in hospital recently I was put in a room on my own, and forbidden to go out in case I was infectious. I felt quite lonely; I had none of my possessions with me, except a book, which someone had recommended.

I looked round the room: it was dismal and drab and there were no pictures or posters on the walls which were uniformly painted grey except for a slab of mustard yellow, my least favourite colour. There was no radio or television or telephone and I felt quite cut off from my familiar world.

Then I picked up my book and began to read. The book is full of beauty, vibrancy and colour. I was taken up into a different place, transported to a world of brilliance and wonder.

Afterwards, I thought of Robert. He is condemned to live in a cell; a room far bleaker and more cramped than mine. Unless he is extremely lucky, he is also condemned to death. And I remember being told again and again, how letters transform the lives of prisoners like Robert. I have a sense of guilt when I write to him, because my life is so comfortable and pleasant. I am twice Robert's age and live in a foreign country. I often wonder how my letters can be of interest to him.

But he writes: *I was very happy and glad to receive your so sweet and loving letter. You really did brighten up my day for me, so very much. You really do know how to put a great big smile on my face!*

In some small way it seem my letters liberate Robert, if only for a short time, just as my book liberated me.

## 4  MARCH

Today, the first of March, came in like a lamb. The air was benign and full of birdsong. I just happened to be in what must be one of the most beautiful places in England, with a view of moorland, scattered small farmsteads and a wide open dale with smaller, narrow, secret valleys branching from it. There is a tree-lined beck running through the middle of the dale, and green fields cover the lower flanks of the moors which are variously: indigo, purple, deep blue, nut-brown, pale green, depending where the sunlight and the shadows fall.

Perhaps, after all, March is the best month. For me, who have always longed impatiently for April and May, this is surely the most promising season, pregnant as it is with even more beauty to come.

## 5   TREASURE

*A reflection on St Luke's Gospel, Chapter 12, verse 22*

There is a piece in Luke's gospel which I particularly like. It is part of Chapter 12. I like it, although I don't succeed at all well in doing as Jesus recommends. "Do not worry about your life and what you are to eat," he says, "nor about your body and what you are to wear." He goes on to exhort us not to set our hearts on such things as food and clothing, but on the things of heaven.

According to the gospel of St Luke,
Jesus said, *'Do not worry*
*about what you are to eat*
*and what you are to wear'.*
He said, *'Consider the lilies of the field,*
*they toil not, neither do they spin,*
*yet Solomon in all his glory,*
*was not arrayed like one of these.'*

I have never been to Galilee,
so have not seen those flowers,
glorious in their beauty.
But I will go and look
at Swaledale's fields of buttercups
that fill a whole valley
with golden light.
And I will gaze at them,
and standing still,
looking for a long time,
I will forget what I am wearing
and fail to notice when I'm hungry,
and even the really big concerns
that normally fret at the edges of my mind,
will drift away.
Then I will understand
where my treasure is,
and so, where my heart is also.

## 6  APRIL

I did not like it,
when T S Eliot wrote,
*"April is the cruellest month,"*
because for all my life,
I have found this time of the year
beautiful beyond expectation,
beyond imagining.
But now,
when I see the first greening of the
hedgerows,
and the tall beeches, naked still
but poised for transformation,
I feel a stab of pain,
seeing in these glad beginnings
transience, impermanence, brevity
and in a word,
inevitability.
This, for me, is the cruelty of April
and a reminder,
to live in the present moment.

## 7  PUSSY WILLOWS

About five weeks ago a friend gave me some 'pussy willows', so called because of their fluffy grey catkins. Some country folk call these strange little flowers 'goslings' because they remind them of geese when they are newly hatched.

Whatever they are called, they are pleasing to look at, especially when combined with daffodils, so when the yellow flowers died, we got another bunch, and later a third.

Now the pussy willows stand alone in the vase on the windowsill, where the catkins catch the light of the sun and turn from grey to silver. And this morning, just when I was wondering whether to throw them out, I noticed small green leaves springing to life along the branches. It seemed like a miracle of resurgent life.

## 8  LOOK!

We were going to see a friend who lives only a few miles away. As we had both been ill, we decided not to take the scenic route which leads across pastoral fields with wide views of the moors beyond, but instead we chose the path along the railway.

It is a narrow, dusty path, with a wire fence next to the track on one side and a tall boarded fence on the other. There were no beautiful vistas on this part of the walk.

As we walked, I was feeling wistful. This Spring, because of illness, we have not been able to go to the woods where millions of daffodils grow, or the bank that is carpeted with primroses at this time of year.

Then my companion, who was behind me, called, "Look!"

I did look, and low to the ground, right up against the fence, and with no visible soil to nourish and support it, was a cluster of exquisite violets.

## 9  GOOD FRIDAY

Today I went to join the Good Friday Walk in our town. We stopped in ten different places to sing and pray, and it was good that all the different Christian traditions were represented.

The town is small and I have lived here for a long time, so I have quite a lot of local friends. As we processed along the streets we passed all sorts of people, tourists and locals going about their business. An agnostic friend noticed me as I walked in silence with the others, following the big cross. She waved and smiled. Further along, another friend who is an atheist, saw me and laughed out loud, though not unkindly.

The experience underlined for me how difficult it is for us to be taken seriously as Christians when we are not in our places of worship. I have some very good friends who are Methodists, Quakers, Anglicans or Catholics, but I also know, and indeed love, some people who find my beliefs odd and absurd. And these same people, like me, strive to be generous, courageous and selfless, and just like me, they fail often.

When the procession was over, I walked home with one of my agnostic friends. She didn't tease me, as I had half expected. She said, "I loved the singing, and the silence. I wished I could have joined in."

# 10 MEMORY

There's a lightness and a brightness in the air today and the southerly wind is dancing. Were it not for my faithful companions, Sciatica and Arthritis, I would be skipping down the street. I find it is one of the challenges of old age, to come to terms with what we have lost: not only dear friends who have died, but our own strength and capacities.

It is hard for me to accept that I will never again turn a cartwheel, or climb a mountain, perhaps no longer be able to wander in the woods looking for the first primrose and the first violet. And I know that as long as my memory holds it will be beyond price. I can still recall moments of simple happiness: the feel of green turf under my feet as I walked over the moors, the delightful icy shock as I plunged into the sea, the sound of the curlew and the warmth of the sun as I lay in the heather, dreaming.

## 11  EXPECTATIONS

Some friends invited me to go with them on a woodland walk. I was very pleased: I love walking through woods and when I was told it was ancient woodland I was even more delighted, knowing it would not be unnaturally clean and tidy.

However, when I got among the trees I no longer felt so sanguine. The sky was overcast and the wood seemed dark and even slightly threatening. It didn't help when I tripped over a half-hidden stump or when my face was scratched by the thorns of unruly branches. It all seemed so gloomy.

We broke through into a small open space. I looked down and literally gasped to see them: thousands of windflowers, purely white and perfect, blooming in that ancient place which was no longer gloomy but full of brightness.

There were plenty of old logs around, so we sat and ate our sandwiches. Hardly tasting them, hardly speaking, just gazing our fill.

Afterwards, I thought about the person people call 'the woman in black'. She walks around the town, not looking at anyone, not speaking to anyone, with not exactly a scowl, but a miserable glare on her face.

One day I decided to go for a walk in the park. The woman in black was sitting on a bench, quite still, her face tight closed. I was wondering if I should try, as I have often tried in vain, to talk with her, to say 'hello', when a small boy, perhaps three years old, came running down the path ahead of his mother. He slowed down as he reached the woman in black, then I saw her face as she looked at him. Her eyes were lit in a wide smile, a smile that didn't leave her face until the little boy and his mother had disappeared from sight.

For me, it was like seeing the windflowers shining in the wood.

## 12  HEALING

I lie in my hospital bed, feeling wistful. My last visitor said "It's such a beautiful day!" I crane my neck, trying to see the blue of the sky and the green of the new leaves bursting from the 'sticky buds' of the horse chestnut tree that I know stands quite near my window, but just out of my line of sight. I strain my ears to hear the sound of excited singing birds, but the world outside this ward is silent to me. The air in here is stuffy: it feels mildly suffocating. I long for the touch on my face of the April breeze that must be tossing the wild daffodils someone had planted at the edge of the hospital grounds.

But why should I feel such discontent? None of the joys of Spring can compare with the blessing of healing, and after all I am here to be healed.

## 13 AWE

Like many people I know, I often find myself thinking about God and asking all sorts of questions about my own faith and the beliefs or non-beliefs of others. I wonder about the nature of God, and I try hard to find satisfactory answers to all my doubts and questions. I want to live by the phrase, 'to thine own self be true', and I think of myself as someone seeking the truth.

But the other day I was startled by a thought, feeling, or moment of understanding, which suddenly struck me. I realised how in my persistent searching and with my puny ideas, I had completely forgotten something central: the awesomeness of God, however we perceive him or her. I realised my own pettiness and was ashamed of my arrogance. I still believe it is right to question and explore, but I feel I should always do so with awe and wonder before the greatness of God who is perfection and love.

## 14 BLUE MOON

I saw a blue moon once.
In the morning, the man on the radio had said,
"Tonight there will be a blue moon."
But there wasn't.
The sky at dusk was blue
but the first I saw of the moon
was bright gold shining through the trees.
And then, round and full,
She sailed slowly into view,
low on the horizon.
She was the colour of flame,
huge beyond belief, and lovelier
for not being blue.

## 15   MARY'S CELEBRATION

Matuka fled from Sierra Leone five years ago and now lives in Middlesbrough with her four daughters, one of whom, nine year old Paula, has severe cerebral palsy. They live in a two-bedroomed house and life is very tough for them. Soon after they arrived, they were helped by a woman called Mary who did everything she could to support them, for example, arranging for Paula to have a commode.

Over the years Matuka watched Mary, seeing how she gave nearly all her time to helping refugees and people seeking asylum, trying to save them from deportation or finding them the food and clothing they needed.

Matuka decided to talk to God about this, and as she told it, God said: 'You must have a celebration for Mary'.

So about fifty refugees helped Matuka to organise a party as an expression of their gratitude. Roughly the same number of British people joined them, and a church hall was decorated with streamers and balloons. There was a lavish amount of food from a variety of nations, music, singing, drumming, dancing and speeches. Mary was incredulous and overwhelmed when she discovered what was happening, but on the night she was humbled and delighted and very surprised to learn how much her efforts to give help and support meant to her friends from overseas.

## 16   RED HOUSE

We have only a few acres now,
the stock: cows, sheep, even the pigs
are gone.
Our sons gone too; all three of them,
Alfred, Billy and Joe.
My Daniel's too old now,
both of us, too old for the new ways.
Still he ploughed well this year;
I see the furrows from my kitchen window,
straight and true,
well, straight enough for an old man.

Our Billy came home in January
and offered to do the outside of the house again.
He's a good lad.
"Whitewash, is it, Mother?" he said
and summat came over me then.
"Nay, our Billy," I said, "paint it red."
We're old, Daniel and me, aye,
but not as set in our ways as you'd think.
The red house looks fine.
I look out of my window
and see the green shoots showing
where Daniel ploughed our field.

## 17  YOUNG GIRL

I stood under the apple tree
and blossom spilled from its branches
falling on me like a blessing.
It felt like a gift from heaven.
Or was it an early promise
of happiness still to come
of pink and white confetti
and bliss on my wedding day?

## 18  DAVY

I was feeling a bit sorry for myself and decided a walk might cheer me up. I thought it was too bad to have toothache and a bad headache on the same day. I was also irritated by the crowds of tourists I was having to fight my way through in the street.

Then I turned a corner and bumped into Davy, smiling as usual.

"How are you?" he asked, and before I could answer, he went on,

"Isn't it a beautiful day? And isn't it good to see all these people enjoying themselves?"

As he spoke, I was looking at Davy. He was dying; all of us, his friends and neighbours knew this. Once a big man with a ruddy complexion, he was now painfully thin, his face drawn and yellow. But he was still smiling, and he held out his hand to shake mine.

"How are you, Petal?" he asked, and I knew he wanted to know so I said,

"I'm fine, thanks, Davy, absolutely fine."

It was true, because my headache and toothache, not to mention my sullen mood, were forgotten.

## 19 A CONCERT

The music was baroque,
    played on harpsichord and violin
with sensitivity.
And we, the audience, the congregation,
sat stiffly in uncomfortable pews,
sedate, polite, attentive, rapt.
No-one snored, cleared her throat or coughed.
We were still, listening to the music.
And all at once, my knees began to jig,
my toes started tapping,
my wild heart longed to leap into the aisle
and dance, to wear a swirling skirt and dance -
 but my tamed heart knew better, I suppose,
I stayed in my place
and behaved appropriately.

## 20  A DIFFERENT KIND OF CONCERT

We were invited to a concert given in aid of people seeking sanctuary in our country. It was a familiar experience: a church hall with rows of uncomfortable seats, a raffle and some light entertainment. Just when we had decided to slip away, [we had a long journey home] the drummers came onto the stage. They were five young African men who had fled the Democratic Republic of Congo in fear of their lives. Some of them had been in England for several years; two were newly arrived. All of them were desperately hoping for permission to stay in Britain.

When they reached the platform, they turned to the audience with big smiles, but as soon as they began to play their faces changed to expressions of fierce concentration. Their fingers moved so fast as to be almost invisible.

We were mesmerised, and now there was no way we were going to leave. I watched those flying fingers and wondered how many of them had been bruised and maimed by torture.

But at the end, the young men, sweating and breathless, stood up, and their big smiles returned to their faces. I felt certain that I would not be able to smile and laugh if my life was full of fear and desperation.

## 21 HOSPITAL

When she was in hospital,
supposedly close to death,
it wasn't the priest that came to see her,
advising repentance,
who spoke to her of God.
It wasn't her family, either.
They came with brave faces,
some of them struggling not to weep, and failing.
Nor was it her friends.
They came laughing,
cheerful and determinedly jolly,
bringing her gifts that were thoughtful,
but useless.
No, it was none of these who spoke to Nell of God.
It was the cleaner,
who put down her mop
and came to sit on the visitor's chair,
gently smiling,
and took her hand
and held it until she fell asleep
for the last time.

## 22 JOY

I remember some of the things that over the years have never failed to bring me joy: a child's first smile, first tooth, first steps and particularly his first real words. And I am thankful that I feel this spontaneous joy, even now in old age, even at times when life is not very easy: if I am walking I feel like skipping when I see the first snowdrop of the year, the first rose of summer, a rainbow, any place and any time. But I wonder if everyone feels like this or if the life experience of some people is so weighed down with sadness or poverty or ill-health or even despair, that this gift of childlike joy is theirs no longer, or perhaps, has never been theirs.

## 23  YORK MINSTER

I am writing this sitting in York Minster. Evening light is slanting through the windows and high-lighting the delicate brasswork on a pulpit, a gold and silver window to my left and part of the carved stonework high above the sanctuary. 'Sanctuary' is the perfect word for what I am feeling now: a few moments of tranquillity and awareness in the midst of all the activity and bustle and stress of my everyday life.

The cathedral soars. The near-whiteness of the stone, and the shape of the Gothic arches direct the eyes of the mind, not perhaps heavenwards; [for who knows where heaven is?] but upwards from everything that clamps us down.

## 24  GOLDFINCH

Oh! The little bird again,
balanced precariously on the clothes line,
endearing, but handsome too.
Look at her: white and black and fawn,
crimson and gold.
She's utterly focussed,
oblivious of everything
except the little fledgling she is feeding
who perches just below her on a twig.

## 25 TURNSTONE

There's something about this little bird. He's not especially attractive or remarkable, except perhaps in the way he moves, which I can only call 'skittering' . I think I like him because he seems so courageous and undeterred to be so far from the beach.

He skitters round and through the legs of passing shoppers. Generally, they don't even notice him, and somehow boots and shoes and sandals don't touch him as he moves adroitly in and out, orange feet skimming over the pavement in all weathers. His search for food seems frenetic; he must be constantly hungry; head down, he tackles the cracks in the concrete, and as far as I can see he never stops. But just sometimes, he spreads his wings and flies. Then I can see more clearly his white belly and the complex patterns of his grey wings. Foolishly, I can even imagine he's looking at me - as if!

## 26 PEACOCK

He cannot soar like an eagle,
sing like a skylark
or endear himself to you
like a cheeky robin or little wren.
No, he's only a great big show-off;
that's all he is. But, I guess,
if I were a dowdy little peahen,
I would fall for him big time
because, there's no denying it,
he's absolutely gorgeous.

# 27  A HAPPY CHILDHOOD

Martha and I met while we were washing up together after a meeting - I forget now what the meeting was about, but I doubt I will ever forget Martha. She was one of those people who is genuinely humble and self-effacing, always shunning the limelight, always getting on with what needs to be done.

I know all this now, but when I first met her she was a complete stranger. We began to talk, as women often do, about their children and their work, though the days of paid work were long gone for both of us.

Martha told me where she lived now and about her son and two daughters. Her husband had died some years earlier. Then I asked her if she had always lived in our town, and her face lit up. She began speaking with enthusiasm.

"Oh, yes," she said, "I have lived here all my life, and I had such a happy childhood. It was wonderful: we lived out in the country but it's all built over now, the town has grown so big. But we had fields all round us and when we were little we played out all day long."

I asked if she had many brothers and sisters.

"Oh yes, there were six of us," she said. "Our Mam was a widow, but she managed. We had no gas, no electricity, no hot water, and we slept in the one bed., all six of us, tip to toe. I remember our Mam taking the bath outside and filling it with snow, then she carried it inside and put it in front of the fire, so that when it was hot we could all have a bath." As Martha was talking her smile broadened and her faded old eyes seemed to sparkle.

"Oh, aye: I had a very happy childhood."

## 28 UNDERGROWTH

June, warm sunshine, nothing to do. I lay in the field, dreaming, then, turning sideways, saw the undergrowth, an unexpected treasure-house of Nature: stems of barley and corn marigolds, careless of their loveliness and yet outshone by poppies. These are the bravest flowers, symbol of gallantry, their myriad seeds mown down year on year by brutal farm machinery, but somehow sprung to life again to bloom, sweetly flamboyant, in the cornfield.

# 29  PARADISE

Perhaps most of us have some idea of Heaven, even those who do not believe in an afterlife. There are certain places, and certain situations, too, which seem to be heavenly, as they are beautiful or ecstatic beyond expectation.

Today I had one such experience of Paradise. In some ways it was quite ordinary, and it occurred on a walk I take often. But I stood, looking at the sea and the sky. There was just a line of white foam edging the sea rather like lace on a petticoat, and in the distance sea and sky touched. The blue of the sea was vivid, intense, brilliant in the sunshine. The blue of the sky was intense too, paler but no less bright. I gazed, and gazed again, and I thought, surely this is Paradise?

## 30  THE WHITE SINNERS

Just for a week, in high summer, we are staying with two of our sons and their wives in the Languedoc, a part of France hitherto unknown to us. The scenery is delightful, lush and green, the villages abound in history and charm and most notably, just at this time of the year, in roses, surely the most English of flowers.

As we were walking through one of the villages, I noticed that one of the streets was named "Les Penitents Blancs". So when we were sitting at a pavement cafe drinking delicious French coffee, I asked my son, who has lived in France for a long time, who were the 'Penitents Blancs'. He didn't know; none of us knew and I resigned myself to never knowing.

But within a minute our other son picked up his smart phone, pressed a button and began to read the intriguing story of Les Penitents Blancs. And I realised that, just as I have been thunderstruck these last few days by the beauty and history of of this place, I am wonderstruck too by the marvels of modern technology. Looking back over more than eighty years, I ask myself, whoever would have thought?! And I thank my God, for all the wonders he has made and keeps making.

## 31   A WAY OF HEALING

It seems to me that in beauty there is often a quality of healing. For this we need time, time to gaze, time to listen intently, time to breathe deeply of the fragrance we find beautiful.

Today, I feel that I have enjoyed an abundance of beauty. I am away from home in a region that is new to me. I have seen the sun rise through a dip in the wooded hills. I have listened to birdsong at daybreak and at twilight looked up at a bright quarter-moon.

I have also stood at the side of a lake and gazed at the peaceful scene in front of me. The lake itself is the palest green, the low hills surrounding it, a shade like navy blue, the sky above thrush-egg blue and high on the southern horizon rise the snowy peaks of he Pyrenees.

It was quiet, and for a while I was almost alone. For a long time I stood there, drinking in the beauty and the peace, and I felt healed.

## 32  TWILIGHT CHORUS

I've always loved the dawn chorus of singing birds. Whether because I am usually occupied around dusk, or whether there really isn't a chorus at dusk in England, I don't know. But as I write, here in the Languedoc in south-western France, now in the early evening, the birds just will not stop singing, not that I want them to! There are many different kinds of song birds, a number of little ones, and even doves joining in with enthusiasm. It is a joy to do nothing else but sit and listen to them.

## 33  CARCASSONNE

When we were staying with our son in the south of France, I very much wanted to go and see Carcassonne. I had seen photographs of its walls which looked magnificent, and I knew that the town had existed in some form or other for over two millennia. I wanted to go there because I knew it to be a place redolent with both history and recurring tragedy which now from the outside gave every appearance of serenity and security.

Carcassonne did not disappoint me. Once inside the walls, I fell in love with the 'city'. It was everything I had imagined, and more. But I was also slightly shocked by the prevalence of what I call 'posh shops', the sort of establishments that sell exquisite things which only the rich can afford. It seemed so incongruous, and even insulting, for a place of such dignity and indeed glory, to be pandering to this kind of blatant commerce. I did not see any beggars there, not even any poor people, yet I wonder how many thousands of beggars and poor people lived there before Carcassonne became a tourist attraction.

For all that, I would love to go there again and spend more time and light another candle in the great church of Saints Nazaire and Celse. And I have to confess that before I left, I bought myself a bar of soap which smells delightfully of lemon and verbena.

## 34  CONTENTMENT

In the Old Testament, there is a description of an old man, his life's work done, sitting under his vine and his fig tree. It is a picture of contentment.

As I write this, I, too, am sitting under a vine, and for all I know there may well be a fig tree nearby, for I am in a land of warm and frequent sunshine.

Like the old man in the bible, I too am old. Moreover, I am blessed not only with children, but my children's children's children. I, too, am content, but I am not yet sleepy and resigned; I still have plans and hopes for the future, and more importantly, involvement in the lives of family and friends.

Above all, I am conscious of a deep welling up of thankfulness for my life and its blessings.

## 35  SUMMER'S NIGHT IN SWALEDALE

At bedtime,
the place was dark,
no lights in the street.
I fell asleep,
but woke some time in the night.
I woke to find my room
curiously bright.
I rushed to the window,
and there was the moon,
perfectly round, and silver,
impassive and serene,
looking at me,
and shining.

## 36 FOXGLOVE

Whenever I see a foxglove, I smile as I remember,
tasting again the sweetness of nostalgia,
savouring the memories of the old days, the old ways:
the careless profusion of flowers in the cottage garden,
the endlessness of sunshine, the delicious smells of summer,
the sound of the beck splashing and bees murmuring,
warm flagstones under my bare feet and raspberries for the picking,
the unclouded happiness of long-ago childhood.

Then, suddenly, war started,
and, as in all wars everywhere,
the dream was shattered,
reality hit.
Everyone rallied, in fortitude and fear,
childhood was over.

And now, after the passing of so many years,
after the shedding of so many tears,
I can smile again whenever I see a foxglove,
revisiting my dream time.

## 37 HAPPINESS

I am lying on a rock by myself in the sunshine
doing nothing,
not even thinking
except perhaps wondering, asking God
if I am going to be with him forever
it could be something like this -
somewhere like this.

I feel the wind soft on my cheek
and the warm sun
the sweet, short-cropped grass tickling my legs.

I can see the great dome of the cloudless sky
and all around the green-gray sculptured
mountains.
I can see no people, no motor cars, no buildings,
only the one house in the middle of this vast
and gentle space,
and everywhere, the little, little flowers.

I can hear the curlew's cry
and the skylark's rapture.

I can hear the children laughing
and the water splashing over the rocks
of the stream by the house ----
For me, here and now,
this is happiness.

## 38  HEDGEROW

The little farmer made a hedgerow,
a cornucopia, a treasure-house,
a home for the honeysuckle, the dog rose,
the blackthorn, the whitethorn and the may,
for the holly and the ivy, the hazel and the
beech,
the old man's beard and the bindweed.
He made it for the small birds, the beetles and
the butterflies,
for the ladybirds and the hedgehogs, the field
mice and the voles.

The big farmer wanted big fields
so he cut down the hedgerow.
Now the sweetness and the scents and the
songbirds
are all gone away.

## 39  BUDDHA AND CHRIST

I look at the small statue of Buddha
in my friend's garden.
He seems so serene in his infinite wisdom
and yet I sense in him
a bottomless capacity
for tenderness.

Strangely, you may think,
he reminds me of the face of Christ
I saw once on a Russian ikon.
He seemed to look right through me,
piercing my soul, and knowing everything,
Those eyes regarded me
with infinite compassion.

## 40 JUDGING

I said I didn't like them much: gladioli,
they made me think of swords
and so, of violence.
In any case, I said, there's something brash
about those vivid colours.
Then you grew these flowers,
pure and delicate and white,
slender-stemmed,
and you said,
'These too, are gladioli.'

## 41 HEATHER

Today I walked across the moor.
I walked for miles and miles,
trudging and tramping through acres and acres,
oceans and oceans, it seemed,
of the pale purple heather.

It's like when the snow comes:
the transformation
from bleakness and dullness
to something overwhelmingly
beautiful.

The purple doesn't speak to me
of royalty.
Its softness speaks to me
of peace.
And I wish - how I wish
it would not fade as summer fades
but stay,
to brighten the land and gladden the heart
until spring comes again.

## 42  NORTHERN LINE

I never thought I would be enraptured
by a railway line.
But I travelled, in high summer,
from Whitby to Ruswarp,
and onwards through Sleights and Grosmont,
Egton, Glaisdale and Lealholm,
Danby and Castleton Moor,
and I stared, enchanted,
as we passed through these little stations
appended to unimportant villages.
I thought,
how can this be so beautiful,
this tunnel of green, green trees full-leaved
enclosing us on either side of the track
and giving us tantalising glimpses all the way
of sloping fields, stone walls,
cattle and sheep grazing?

## 43  PEBBLE

I felt stressed, 'frayed at the edges' and muddle-headed. So instead of doing anything about it, I decided to go out into the garden and sit quietly for a while in that place of loveliness and peace, with only foxgloves and bumblebees and roses and small birds to distract me. It was an ideal situation for practising mindfulness. So I sat there, alone and at peace.

But it was no use. There were just so many things to do and sort out in the house, unless I did something about them and organised some priorities. I stood up ready to move indoors, when my eye fell on a pebble, quite an ordinary gray pebble, that was lodged inside a flower pot. I paused and looked, and looked again at the pebble. I saw how smooth it was, and thought of the winds and waves that had been moulding its shape for thousands of years. I thought of the hymn 'O God, our help in ages past', and I remembered the line 'Time, like an ever-rolling stream, bears all its sons away' and I understood how petty and unimportant those concerns, which had seemed so urgent, were. Yes, I would need to prioritise and tackle them soon, but there was no need to feel so frantic and obsessive.

I sat down and went on focussing my attention on the pebble.

## 44  BLUE SKIES

Now, in the middle of July, the sun is shining day after day from a cloudless sky. I am wearing my comfortable old summer frock and I feel an especial happiness as I walk along the path where Lady's Mantle brushes against my bare legs. To my surprise, I find I am singing aloud, [though not loudly!] a song that has come into my head from my childhood long ago.. The words go something like this:

*Glad that I live am I*
*that the sky is blue,*
*glad for the country lanes*
*and the fall of dew.*
*All that we need to do,*
*be we low or high,*
*is to see that we grow*
*nearer the sky.*

I remember the words of this song so clearly, after many, many years, and I find it has the same effect on me now as it did when I was nine or ten years old. As a child, I loved the joyousness of the song and we sang it whole heartedly. The idea that we don't have to **do** anything, anything good or brave or useful, felt so reassuring all those years ago. But then the uncomfortable doubts began to nag: surely I can't simply be happy? I have to do something, achieve something....

And now, today, nearly eighty years later, I find I have hardly grown free of this seemingly inherent prick of conscience, a kind of puritanism, perhaps, that impels me to be 'doing'.

I know full well that Theresa told us that we are to be the hands and feet of God among our fellow human beings, and like St Francis, I pray to be an instrument of peace. It is up to me to work, with love, for justice in the world.

But I also believe, that on a blessed summer's day, it's good to be just glad, glad to be alive, glad that the sky is blue.

## 45  TWO GIRLS

The girl with a small crucifix on a silver chain round her neck walked up to the top of the cliff to see the sun rise over the sea. She saw that another girl was standing there, wearing a hijab.

The girl in the hijab said: "Why are you here?"

"I'm here to watch the sun rise," said the girl with the crucifix, "and to worship my God in the holiness of beauty."

"Me too," said the girl with the hijab.

## 46  PERSONALITY

This week two people kindly brought me flowers. The first one gave me a small pink rose, its petals still tightly furled. The second one presented me with three big sunflowers, flamboyant and surely making a statement about sunshine and life.

I placed the little rose in a delicate glass, the sunflowers in my big brown jug, and I enjoyed them both. As I looked at them I thought about people I know: some who are reserved, quiet, gentle and wise delight me; others are exuberant, uninhibited, feisty and frank, and they delight me too.

But as I thought about this, I realised that whereas there is a clear contrast between the rose and the sunflowers, in reality very few people are entirely inward looking or completely extrovert. More interestingly, each one of us has a complex personality which reveals itself according to circumstances.

Much as I appreciate my rose and my sunflowers, I feel grateful that we as human beings are creatures of such variety.

## 47  ABOUT GOD

I always seem to be worrying about God - him, her...
I wonder of he smiles, knowing how we struggle
to work it all out, to understand.
I wonder if he laughs
when he hears the theologians and the scientists
puzzling and squabbling about his existence.

## 48  WHITBY YARD

Hidden away in the Yard
the song of small birds wakes us
before the seagulls start to squawk and scream.
The old houses face each other across the grass
and steps climb steeply between the cottages.
Surely no architect has ever planned
this pleasing muddle
of gentrified fishermen's homes.
All the outside lavatories
are gleaming sheds now,
and black smoke doesn't smirch the sky
any more.
There was grime and poverty here once,
there's comfort and prettiness today,
but history lingers in the faded bricks,
in the worn old beams,
and the butterfly hinges.

## 49   AFTER FRANCIS

Many people think it was St Francis who told his followers to preach the good news of Jesus Christ, "if necessary in words". And it was certainly the pope who took his name who drew people to the love of God when on Holy Thursday, soon after his election, he went into a prison and washed the feet of a Muslim woman.

This action was surely more efficacious as evangelisation than any 'worthy' words would have been, and held within it the implication that the indwelling of God is everywhere: in popes and in criminals, in people of every faith and none, even in women!!

## 50  FADING

In the afternoon, I usually sit in my chair. Sometimes I try to meditate or pray, sometimes I simply sit.

If my eyes are open, at this time of year, late summer, their focus is nearly always on a rose placed in a glass on the mantlepiece. Apart from their loveliness and fragrance, our roses have beguiling names like New Dawn, Natural Beauty and Compassion.

The particular rose Chris picked for me two days ago was Compassion, my favourite. But he hesitated before cutting it because there was a bud close to the flower and he was afraid it might not open. However, today, I see the rose is faded almost to white, and the petals are about to fall, whereas the bud, now rosy and opening to its fulness, leans just behind the flower, making me think of a small child safe on the back of its mother as she labours in the fields of a hot and distant country.

The roses seem like a metaphor for life: the old must fade, losing their vigour and their appeal, the young will grow and flourish

# 51   COURT CASE

The atmosphere in the courtroom was tense, frightening even. It was going to be literally a matter of life or death. John's fate hung in the balance. The ten of us who had come to support him by our presence, all sat in silence, waiting for the judge to appear. We love John and were convinced of the validity of his claim for asylum, but we were powerless. My guess is that each of us: atheist, agnostic or Christian, was intent on prayer.

John has waited seven years for this moment. He sat very still,with his head bowed, waiting. When the door opened, we all stood. The judge said, "Good morning', sat down and shuffled his papers. Then he looked up  and spoke to us.

"I'm very sorry," he said, "but this case will have to be adjourned. I find that some papers are missing."

It wasn't so much the anticlimax; it was more that John had invested so much hope and had endured so much pain waiting for this decision which would have been crucial.

When we came out of the room John couldn't smile; he couldn't even speak. He knew, as we all did, that this meant more months of waiting, more days of desperation, more nightmares.

There is no alternative; he, and we, can only continue to wait and to pray.

## 52  SORROW

It is nearly September, a balmy day. I climbed to the top of the cliff and gazed and gazed again, unable to look away from the placid blue of the sea and the beauty of my surroundings, that miraculous beauty which sometimes stirs the spirit as well as the senses, perhaps what people mean by 'a tug at the heart strings'.

Eventually I came down and walked along the street to see my friend Violet who knows she is facing death. It was a short, quiet visit, with love expressed between us. I returned home slowly, and looked up to where the Morning Glory, trailing round the doorway, should have been in full bloom. But we had not watered it enough and all the buds were tightly shut. I have poured water lavishly over the roots, but I fear it is too late.

I was chastened by the loveliness and sorrow of this day.

## 53  MORNING GLORY

Over a week ago, I wrote a rather sad piece in which I noted the failure of our climber, Morning Glory, to flower this year because we had forgotten to water it. Over the blue front door and against the faded old brick wall, there was a row of stiff, tight buds. The stems leading up to them looked withered and the leaves brown. It was a sorry sight. Chris watered it that evening.

And then this morning, he called me into the garden, sounding excited, and pointing to the door, he said 'Look!'. There were four perfect flowers, their pale blue trumpets open wide, and now there seems no reason why the rest of the buds won't open too.

Perhaps this seems a trivial thing to get so worked up about. After all it's only a flower, a flower in a garden where many blooms flourish. And, in any case, the flowers only live for a day.

But for us, it seemed to be a symbol of the hope that never dies.

## 54  FALL

It is Fall now.
The leaves are falling,
falling, falling,
crimson, scarlet, carmine, rose,
russet, bronze and palest gold.

How can it be
that sadness is so beautiful?
The leaves are falling,
floating, fluttering,
twisting, turning,
sliding, spiralling,
diving, dancing
down.

How can it be
that facing certain death,
Autumn is so brave?

## 55 STAYING

They have all gone now,
all five of my children,
gone to live in the south.

"It's warmer," says Kate,
"it would suit you, Mother."
"I like to be in the swim" says Joe,
"I like to be at the cutting edge" says Rob,
"I love to be anonymous" says Mike,"
with a great sigh of satisfaction.
Frankie, my wise one, says nothing,
only smiles and shakes her head.
She understands.

I am staying here
where, in Winter, the bitter winds
blow in from the chill gray sea,
battering us in their ferocity,
and Spring comes late, but lovelier for that
and change comes very slow.
I am staying here where I belong.
I've planted my roots
and people know me.

# 56 WILDFIRE

The wildfire was terrible, beautiful. Nothing could stop the ferocity of the flames and their wind-driven speed. The fire engines came lumbering over the moor, but the men stood at a distance, shaking their heads. They were lamenting their helplessness in the face of such overwhelming power, some of them, perhaps, seeing something of the wonder and glory of the sight, all of them thankful that this was happening far from any human habitation.

When it was all over, we went to look. The hillside was no longer green moorland but just a great black scar on the landscape. Someone, perhaps it was a local lad from the nearest farm, was the one to spot it, the peculiar stone. As soon as word got out, the experts arrived: archaeologists, historians, photographers, men and women who looked important and single-minded. The big stone was covered in ancient writings, indecipherable to lay people, but of huge significance to history and archaeology. It was measured and photographed from every angle. We all went home, and some time after dark, people returned and buried the stone deep in the ground some distance away, lest anyone should stumble upon it.

It seemed altogether strange that the great fire which had destroyed so much had brought this curious treasure to light.

## 57 LEVERET

Afterwards,
when it was all over,
I saw the young leveret,
crouched, hunched,
on the edge of the black desolation.
He didn't flee like hares do
at the merest glimpse of a human;
he just stayed there, watching.
I wondered if he had seen what I saw,
felt as I felt:
amazed, astonished and stunned
by the terrible beauty of the flames
and the fury of the fanning wind.
I wondered, if like me,
he mourned the loss of the placid green hillside
where I had walked and he had played.
And I wondered, foolishly perhaps,
if he could see beyond the utter devastation
and shared my hope
of life renewed.

58 THE LIME TREE

When we got back from our walk, I pulled a comb through my hair and a small gold leaf fluttered down to the floor. I picked it up, looked at it, and smiled, remembering. The day had not seemed propitious for walking. It was mid-November, the sky overcast. The fields were bare with little colour, the hedges leafless. Our walk took us on a downhill path through woodland, and on a sudden turn in the slippery, muddy path, we saw it: the golden tree. It blazed with light in that sunless place, a young lime tree with every leaf shining.

In the moment of seeing it, I was startled with wonder, but when back at home, I looked at the small leaf and thought about gold. I thought of the Spanish churches, magnificent with gold, the price of which was the slaughter of innocent native Americans. I thought of the Trump Tower in New York with its huge 'waterfall' - a wall of gold down which water cascades, a statement of wealth. And I thought of the little lime tree.

## 59  ROOSTING

At dusk the rooks are coming home to roost,
to settle in their own familiar trees
their great black phalanx flies across the vale
with the fair backdrop of a sunset sky.
The rook's an unattractive bird,
ungainly, harsh of voice, cawing unceasingly,
but rooks together, a parliament soaring,
well, that's another story.

## 60  WIDOW

It isn't about sex,
and maybe, not even about love.
It's not about this deadly cold
piercing my bones under the double duvet.
But I would give anything,
everything,
to feel the pressure of your old back
on my old back,
again.

## 61  REMEMBERING

Remember me in the good times,
the loving and the laughing.
Remember our wonder
at the beauty of our world.
Remember me in the small things,
familiar everyday things.
Remember all we shared
of struggle, disappointment, hope,
joy in our children and our friends.
Remember me, but learn to live
strong in courage strong in faith,
giving as you always gave,
and smile when you remember me.

## 62  HANKERING

You might think
    that now I am old and grey
[though not yet full of sleep]
I would hanker after colour
and music and dancing.
And so I do,
in the mornings, on the good days.
But mostly, I long only
to listen to the silence
and the sometimes sounds of the small birds
or the trees or the rain,
and I wish only
to look at the bare white walls of my room
and see, beyond, through the window,
the curve of the mist-blue hill.

# 63  CRUCIFIXION

On our bedroom wall we have two crucifixes. One of them we gave to each other on our wedding day, a very long time ago. It was made by a Polish refugee artist then living with the Carmelite monks at Aylesford. I remember that we both thought it was beautiful. The figure of Christ, moulded in bronze, is fixed to a plain wooden cross. It is graceful, and the face of Jesus benign and calm.

Some forty years later, our second little crucifix was given to us by a friend who had visited the people of Rwanda shortly after the terrible genocide of 1994. It had been made by one of the Tutsi survivors, who had survived, but had nothing. Making such simple crosses was a way to earn money for food.

When I want to meditate on the passion and death of Jesus, it is not the bigger crucifix I choose to look at. It is the little one, which is less that four inches tall, not really a cross at all, but a crudely shaped figure with arms outstretched, that brings to mind the raw suffering of Jesus, and the raw suffering of victims of cruelty and torture all over the world. Since I read about the reality of crucifixion in Fr Pagola's powerful book, "Jesus, an Historical Approximation", my beautiful crucifix no longer draws my eyes and thoughts as it once did. It is the small one which speaks to me of loss and love, forgiveness and hope.

## 64  WEATHER

This morning we walked along the beach. It was a day like no other; it always is. Today it was face-stingingly cold, but bright overhead. Sometimes the sun shone, sometimes it stayed hidden. The wind, frolicking, teasing, kept us guessing, tossing the clouds, tossing the waves, tossing my hair with wild abandon, and then the sun was shining again and the sky placid. I thought how I love the weather, love its unpredictability, and felt glad to live in a place where no one day is like another.

## 65  LAZARUS

The story of Dives and Lazarus haunts me, especially the picture of the poor man, Lazarus, covered in sores, who longed to fill himself with the scraps that fell from the rich man's table.

When our friends Mike and Sue came back from their holiday in a small town in Somerset, we invited them round for an evening to tell us all about it. They had certainly had an interesting time, enjoying all sorts of different experiences, but one small incident Sue described, struck me more than anything else. "We were hungry" she said, "and looking for somewhere to eat. We turned up a long steep street and from the corner of my eye I noticed a man sitting crumpled on the pavement. He was dirty and dishevelled, his head bowed. We walked on, up the hill, and found a cafe where we ordered sandwiches. They looked delicious, but we both realised at once that we wouldn't be able to eat them: they were much too big.

I sighed and said, 'I hate throwing food away!' But Mike called the waitress and asked for a box. Then he put half of each sandwich into the box. He said, 'Let's give them to the homeless man at the bottom of the street.'

I was apprehensive. I thought the man might be angry and say he only wanted money. But it wasn't like that. Mike explained that we hadn't been able to eat it all and the man looked up and for a moment started in surprise, then took the box, opened it and gave us both a warm smile. "Thank you" he said.

And listening to Sue, I remembered Lazarus.

## 66  UNCLE VERNON

I went to visit Uncle Vernon in the Residence for Retired Gentlemen which is his home. I didn't want to go; I doubted if he would recognise me. But there seemed to be nobody else: no other relation, no friend.

I found him in a room that was horrible. It stank to high heaven, and noting this, I cynically felt sorry for the angels. There were several men there, each slumped in his chair in a different attitude. Nobody spoke; and only one had his eyes open. He looked at me and smiled a toothless grin. Nervously I returned his smile, but he no longer seemed to see me.

Uncle Vernon was in the far corner, fast asleep and snoring gently. He was dressed, like always in a three-piece suit with a sombre grey tie. Guiltily I remembered how we used to laugh at him all those years ago. He had no idea how to relate to children, and cruelly, we mocked him. We thought him pompous and weird.

Now, though, he looked crumpled and shrunk. I spoke his name and he looked up. His eyes were blank. I sat on a chair next to him and took his hand. He didn't pull away. I smiled and said, "Uncle Vernon, don't you remember me?"

But there was no response.

I wasn't sure what to do. I longed to escape that smelly, stifling room. But I had driven a hundred miles to see Uncle Vernon, and I could hardly spend only two minutes in his company.

And so I decided to stay. I sat there holding his hand for a very long time. I thought, what a waste of time. I thought, I am hating every minute of this.

Then I looked across to the window. Outside there was a big garden, and across the lawn a line of tall trees. It was early November, mid afternoon. The sun was shining on the brilliant leaves that had not yet fallen, and the wind was tossing the branches in a wild dance. Beyond, the sky was cloudless, blue like summer. Somehow it was unbearably beautiful.

We sat in the room together, Uncle Vernon and I, holding hands and silently staring ahead. I can't know what he thought or what he felt, but in those moments, I felt torn apart, by rage at the way old people are treated, and wonder at the loveliness of Nature.

Then there was the clatter of a trolley outside, and teacups rattling. The door opened and a cheery voice called, "Come along, now, boys, it's time for tea!"

Gently I slipped my hand from Uncle Vernon's. I tried in vain to meet his eyes. I walked out of that room and that house. I got into my car and fled.

## 67  FOREVER

If you love me,
don't give me bright green peridots,
purple amethysts or golden amber.
Don't give me diamonds
which are not for ever.
Give me instead a bright green pebble
from the shores of Iona
washed by those high and  holy seas
since forever.

## 68 STARS

It only happened once, in all the long years. I was on a northern island, stumbling my way along the path because the darkness was so thick, so complete. Then I looked up, and saw the sky alive with stars, brilliant, solid, no space between them. I could not move, but gazed upwards, astonished, delighted and drawn to worship, acutely aware of my own littleness.

# 69  MELODY

My granddaughter told me about her friend, Melody Brown. Her father had disappeared from her life when she was two, so she had no memory of him, but had grown up happily with her mother. Then, when Melody was sixteen, Mrs Brown became seriously ill. Although she was still at school, Melody spent all her free time trying to care for her mother.

Then, one dreadful day, Mrs Brown was taken to a hospice, and Melody was told she had only a few days to live. On the third day, she was taken out of school and driven to the hospice, where she was told to go and say her last words to her mother.

When she came out of that room, Melody couldn't speak, nor could she stop the flow of tears running down her cheeks. She was driven away on her own, and she didn't look back. But after a few minutes she glanced up at the sky, and saw an aeroplane, glinting silver in the sun and soaring up and away out of sight.

Perhaps no one else could understand this, but Melody felt immeasurably comforted. There was no logic or sense in her reaction, nor was she a 'religious' child, but in that moment it seemed to her that her mother's spirit was being lifted up to a place of welcome and joy.

## 70  COFFEE AFTER CHURCH

On Sundays, after the service, people meet for coffee in the church hall. Dora nearly always goes, it's a chance to meet up with friends and have a good chat. Elaine hardly ever comes: she has too many commitments. So when she walked into the hall last Sunday, Dora was delighted. She stood up and called out 'Elaine!', beckoning her to come and join herself and Dorothy and May at their table, and noticing that people at the other tables were doing the same thing. Undoubtedly Elaine was very popular, but Dora thought of her as her own particular friend.

Elaine smiled round at everybody, then took a cup of coffee and to Dora's surprise and disappointment, walked across to join the strange woman sitting on her own. This person was a puzzle to everyone. For the last few weeks she had appeared at the coffee morning every Sunday and had sat by herself. There was something odd about her. She had a rather serious expression and always wore the same shabby clothes and no make-up.

However, when Elaine sat down next to her, Dora didn't hesitate. With an apologetic smile to Dorothy and May, she walked over to join Elaine and the stranger.

The woman, whose name was Meg, turned out to be interesting and amusing too. She was new to the town and lived alone, her husband and young daughter both dead. She had travelled extensively: in India, Africa and the Far East, mostly working in refugee camps, and she had stories to tell. Recently, illness had forced her to retire and now, at sixty, she was trying to find a job and earn a living.

As the three women were still talking, Dora and Elaine mainly engrossed in listening to Meg, the lights in the hall were suddenly dimmed and a cheery voice called "Time, ladies, please!" They looked up and saw that everyone except the caretaker had left.

"Good heavens!" Dora said. "Oh, Joe, I'm so sorry. We just got carried away!" They quickly collected their things and made for the door.

"Please come back next week, Meg." "Yes, I will, Dora," she said, "I will, gladly. I'll look forward to it. It's funny, but I'd decided not to come again. I've come here for the last five weeks on the trot, you see, and not met anyone till today. Then Elaine......" she stopped.

"Where is Elaine?" she asked.

Dora smiled sadly. "She must have slipped away," she said. "Elaine's always busy with one thing or another. But do please come again next week. It will be great to see you."

## 71  CREATION

I am sitting in the sunshine on a bright summer morning, and thinking. I am thinking about the wonderful variety and diversity of Creation. I think of wild places , of deer and hares, giraffes and kangaroos. I think of our garden, with its slugs and butterflies, not to mention its roses and its weeds. I think of young Ian, who has cerebral palsy, and Wendy with her painfully thin body and heavily made-up face. I think, with love, of Polly, whose plain features are transfigured by her smile. And I wonder at God's tenderness and generosity, and, it goes without saying, his creativity!

## 72  NOT FORGETTING

The night before Jesus died he took a piece of bread, broke it and shared it among his friends. Then he said, 'Do this in memory of me.' I find it poignant to think of the trillions of women and men who have heeded these words through the generations, and faithfully remember him in the breaking of bread.

When my good friend Patrick died, I went to his funeral. Attached to every Order of Service was a small white envelope. I opened it, and inside I found seeds of a plant called 'Forget-me-not'. Patrick was asking that when we sowed these seeds and later saw the small blue flowers bloom, we would remember him.

## 73  FRAGRANCE

This morning I bumped into a friend. For fear of embarrassing her I will not use her name but call her Violet. She has been terminally ill for months and when we hugged I could feel the frail bones of her body.

When we parted I was surprised to smell a subtle fragrance on my coat. I don't wear scent, but this perfume lasted for hours.

Soon afterwards I met a mutual friend, Sarah, and told her I had met Violet.

"She is the most generous person I know" Sarah said.

I said. "She is the bravest person I know."

And we agreed that Violet is the most cheerful person we know.

I doubt if the fragrance that lingered on my clothes was a spiritual manifestation, but I do hope that something of Violet has rubbed off on me, so that I may become more generous, braver, and unwaveringly cheerful, as she is.

## 74  CHARLOTTE

I belong to a group of 'worthy' people, not the great and the good, [though we could perhaps claim to be civilised and tolerant, and certainly serious]. We are priests, readers, churchwardens and one or two 'thinking' laity.

There are twelve in the group, nine men and three women, [as you might expect], Nancy, and Charlotte and me.

We talk about Scripture, Church History, Dogmas and Councils, not to mention the decline in church attendance and the problem of the Buildings.

The women say little, but when they do, it is usually about humanity, and kindness, and the beauty of Creation [as you might expect].

We often meet in Charlotte's beautiful house, and after the discussion, she gives us a splendid meal.

We are all grateful: and kiss her and thank her as we say goodbye, and leave her to the washing up
[as you might expect].

*In case you may wonder, reader, why I don't stay and help with the washing up,*
*it is because I depend on one of those men to drive me home.*

## 75  ELLEN PAYNE

We stood in the cold, waiting for a bus that didn't come. We are well into our eighties, both with painful backs, and we longed to be able to get away from the chill wind and to sit down. When at last the bus driver drew up, a gang of school children emerged from nowhere and pushed in front of us. Then, all at once, a young girl noticed us. With a gentle smile she beckoned to us to get on the bus ahead of her.

This may seem a small thing but that simple gesture brought tears to my eyes, tears of gratitude and relief. We're unlikely ever to see this girl again, but we asked her name, and it's a name we'll remember for a long time: Ellen Payne.

## 76  RETIREMENT

Joan worked all her life with people with disabilities, children and adults, the physically and mentally afflicted. She befriended them, took them on holidays, listened to them, taught them and nursed them. She loved them and was loved in return.

But eventually ill health forced Joan to retire. After so many years of lifting people in and out of wheelchairs her back had finally given way. Her life changed dramatically and she was forced to live at home, spending most of her time reading, listening to music or watching television.

Then one day the minister of her church invited her to attend a healing service. Two strong men came to collect her and lifted her into a minicab where a smiling young woman made sure she was comfortable. At the church she was lifted into a chair and wheeled inside to join a row of people who were in chairs like herself, old like herself.

She watched more strong, smiling people, busy about the church, helping. And, far more than retirement itself, this was a shock to Joan's sense of identity. She thought: "All my adult life I've been like them. I was a helper, now I'm being helped."

"Joan Hemingway," she chided herself. "You may not like it, but this is your lot now. I guess you'll have to learn to accept it."

And as she was being wheeled out of church, she thought: "My back is still hurting; that hasn't changed, but maybe acceptance is a kind of healing."

My friend Myfanwy was a gentle eccentric. She always wore colourful clothes, long patterned skirts and faded velvet jackets, but she was not in the least flamboyant or anxious to be noticed, not by the time I knew her.

On the contrary, she was self-effacing; she chose to live alone, far from civilisation, at the bottom of a deep green valley. Her house was old and built of Cotswold stone, her garden overflowed with flowers. She never locked her door, in case a passerby needed shelter, although as there was only a rough track which ended at her cottage, the number of passers-by was limited. Myfanwy spent her days walking in the fields and woods, praying and painting.

Growing up in South Wales, she had trained to be a teacher, but before taking up a post, she had told her parents that she was leaving for London. Her father was dismayed.

"If you do that, you will have burnt your bridges!" he warned. But Myfanwy replied,

"I can't wait to turn and see all my bridges blazing!"

As it turned out, in her long life she saw many bridges burning: she worked as a dancer and an artist's model, she experienced serious poverty, marriage, the birth of her children, bereavement, tragedy and loss. Now in her eighties she was at peace.

One day I said to her, "Your face is beautiful."

Her reply was characteristically sharp. "Don't say that! It isn't true."

I looked at the deep wrinkles, the brown blotches, the yellowing skin and the gray, straggling long hair, and I said: " Myfanwy, it is true."

After her funeral, one of her sons showed us a portrait of Myfanwy in her early twenties. It was painted by an artist who became internationally famous. Even she could not have denied that she was beautiful then, and sixty years later there was still a compelling radiance in her face.

## 78  SEESAW

Yesterday I was with a woman friend who was brimful of happiness and the sense of something pretty wonderful achieved. I wonder how long it will last, for her.

I spent the rest of the day with another friend who is suffering intensely. I wonder if time will ever heal her? Will the love of friends bring her comfort?

Life is rich in contrasts. This May morning I am looking out at a garden which is alive with blossom and colour. Above the sky is a monochrome grey and rain is tumbling in cold, heavy showers.

Sometimes, there is so much contrast in life that I feel that I'm bumping up and down on a seesaw.

## 79  REFLECTION

It is December, and on this very cold morning I was crossing the river at about eight o'clock. Ahead of me, in the east, I could see that the sun would soon be rising over the hill, but then I looked back to the west, and saw the glorious light of its reflection already shining over the town from the walls of the tall cliff top houses.

I thought of the phrase 'reflected glory' and then I wondered how much we reflect one another. Does the presence of a gentle spirit soften me? Or the joyous noise of happy children lift my own heart in response? I think so.

As Alison set off for the supermarket, it was so cold that she was wearing her warmest coat, a woolly hat, a scarf and thick gloves. Nearing the store she saw that Bet, her Bosnian friend, was standing a few yards from the entrance, shivering and clutching her bundle of Big Issues. Bet was frail a young woman, slight and pale, wearing a thin coat over her cotton dress. When she caught sight of Alison, she smiled.

They hugged each other, Alison flinching as she always did to feel the fragility of Bet's body.

"You're so cold and so thin!" she said. "How many copies have you sold this morning?"

Bet's smile was rueful. "None, so far," she said.

"Why don't you step inside the store?" Alison suggested.

But Bet shook her head.

"Not allow. Man shouting at me."

Alison was enraged. She strode into the supermarket and asked to see the manager.

He was very polite until he heard her request.

"Listen!" he said, "we've had loads of complaints about her from customers. They say she makes them feel uncomfortable. Why can't she go back to her own country and beg there? She's lucky we let her stand so near the store."

Alison knew where Bet lived: in a tenement where she shared one room with her old mother, her crippled younger sister and the sister's twin babies. There were only two beds so Bet slept on the floor.

Uncomfortable? Alison thought angrily. People like those precious customers don't know what 'uncomfortable' means! She bought a mug of take away coffee and a chocolate bar and took them out to Bet.

"I'd like to buy a Big Issue, please," she said.

"But you bought yesterday."

"I know, this is for a friend" Alison said, smiling and trying to hide the anger and sadness she felt.

## 81  DIVINITY AT CHRISTMAS

Human beings are very good at worship. Think of cathedrals, temples, mosques: all that glorious imagination and painful toil through the ages.

Think of the Moslem, who breaks off whatever he is doing, and falls on this knees in the dust to pray.

Think of the Irish farmer, who breaks off whatever he is doing to heed the Angelus.

And wonder, on this Christmas day, if there isn't a spark of Divinity in our universe that can never be extinguished.

## 82 HOME

It's so nice to be home for Christmas,
isn't it?
Is it?
Surely it depends on the home?
It might be a castle
or a cottage
or a cardboard box.
It might even be a cattle shed.

## 83  GOLD

*[Looking at the cliffs at sunset from the East Pier at Whitby]*

One of the three wise men, it is said,
gave the infant Jesus
a present of gold,
symbol of wealth and power.
But I can't help wondering,
had times and circumstances
been different,
might he not have preferred
to play on this pier
and gaze at these golden rocks?

## 84 SNOW

It seems to me that snow is like Marmite; people either love it or hate it.

One of my first memories - I suppose I was about three - is of waking up to snow and feeling enchanted, excited, impatient to be out of the house and in it.

My mother firmly said No. The snow was too deep and too cold. It was out of the question. But I wouldn't stop pleading. I guess I felt then that there was a magical world out there waiting to be explored, and nothing would deter me, not even my redoubtable, sensible mother. At last she relented.

"You can go, then, if you promise not to let the snow over the tops of your wellingtons."

I promised, and meant to keep my promise, but the sheer joy of tramping along through the beautiful white stuff made me forget. I went as far and as fast as I could, delighting in the crisp, cold air my mother feared so much, and of course, filling my boots with snow.

So many years later, I still love the snow. Of course I am concerned about the dangers of travelling in icy conditions, about children missing school and working parents losing pay because they have to stay at home. But none of this detracts from the awe I still feel when I gaze at my world transformed, the landscape beautiful, and unsmirched, the trees sparkling where the sun strikes their laden twigs and branches. I still long to run out there and fling myself into the drifts, regardless of filling my 'wellingtons'.

## 85  TRICIA IN BETHLEHEM

It's Christmas, and I am struggling not to feel sorry for myself. A chest infection has knocked the stuffing out of me, and I have no energy, no appetite.

But as I rest here, there are constant reminders of how absurd it is to indulge in self-pity. One is a very beautiful soft blanket, woven in rich reds and purples and blues, a gift from Tricia; another is a peace lily, graceful, sturdy, the least troublesome of house-plants. It too, is a present from Tricia.

Today, at Christmas, Tricia is in Bethlehem, of all places to be at this time. She is there as a peace worker, one of a team of EAPPI [Ecumenical Accompaniment Programme in Palestine and Israel] women and men, who have gone to Palestine to befriend and accompany [without political involvement] people whose suffering is far more real, deep and lasting than any chest infection.

Two or three days a week, Tricia gets up around four o'clock in the morning and walks down to the nearest Checkpoint, to stand by and observe the long sad stream of Palestinians trying to get through the barrier guarded by Israeli soldiers. They **must** get through for work, for a hospital visit, for whatever makes it imperative for them to make this humiliating and frightening journey.

At Christmas, in Bethlehem, very early in the morning, it is very cold, bitterly cold for the workers, the young soldiers, for Tricia.

I wrap my beautiful blanket more closely round my knees.

Clemence is a middle-aged Palestinian widow living in Bethlehem, in the house where she was born. One morning she woke up to a strange and frightening sound. She looked out and saw a great yellow bulldozer churning up her garden just outside her window. It had uprooted her olive trees and her little garden was destroyed.

Soon afterwards, on the other side of the great Wall that had been built, Clemence's daughter gave birth to her first baby. Like any other grandmother she couldn't wait to see her daughter and give her help. But the Israeli authorities refused to give her a permit. Now, as a Christian, she is allowed to visit her daughter and grandchild just twice a year, at Easter and Christmas.

But Clemence is not cowed, nor is she resigned. She is not even angry. Instead, she is doing all she can to promote justice. When asked to put into words what she wanted, she said: "Peace and justice is all we ask, and to have our dignity. Our hope comes from our faith in God, our belief in non-violence and the power of love."

## 87　HEAVEN FOR EVERYONE

I was made very happy today by the words of Pope Francis. I read that in an informal sermon to Vatican employees, he had said that Christ has redeemed the whole of humankind. Someone asked, "Father, even the atheists?" "Even them" he said, "the Lord has redeemed all of us, everyone, with the blood of Christ, everyone, not just Catholics, everyone!"

I find this very consoling remembering how, over hundreds of years, various factions have claimed that theirs is the only true faith, condemning others to eternal damnation. How could this be so, since all that we know of compassion and love is of God?

## 88 STARING

It was a peaceful evening, balmy and cloudless, with very few people about. There was only a gentle breeze and it was pleasantly warm.

I walked down to the pier and decided to sit for a while. I read the plaque on the bench I was about to use. Under the name of the person commemorated, was a quote from the poet W. H. Davies. It read:

*"What is this life, if full of care*
*we have no time to stand and stare."*

How right he was! I thought, but because I was tired, I opted to **sit** and stare.

I was in the place where the river widens as it flows into the sea. I saw that the breeze was playing on the little waves, and the sun was making them sparkle. I gazed for a while, at first content, then filled with wonder. I was looking down at the river, but it was like looking up at a night sky that was alive with zillions of stars. So I stayed for a long time.

## 89 RACISM

I hesitated before introducing David to the twins, Megan and Ross, who are five years old, realising how different he would seem from anyone they had ever met before. But on reflection I felt pretty confident there would be no problem. So I called the children over and told them that our friend had come to stay and would like to meet them. He was in the house and would be coming out. They stood close together, waiting. I was a little nervous, wondering if they would turn and run,or simply look embarrassed. David came out, smiling. He is six foot six inches tall, and very black.

'This is David," I said.

The twins eyes shone as they looked up at him. From the expression on their faces, you might have thought they had had a surprise encounter with a fairy King, or, at the very least, a Big Friendly Giant, which is of course exactly what David is.

"I am Megan" she told him happily.

"And I am Ross" said he.

And I thought, "Racism?"
It seems as though there is is no such
conception in the minds of the innocent.

## 90 FORGIVENESS

When he is describing the crucifixion of Christ, St Luke tells us that at the height of his suffering, Jesus cried out, "Father, forgive them, they do not know what they are doing."

To us, such generosity of spirit. such a measure of understanding and compassion, seems incredible. In such circumstances, how could he have spoken those words?

I think the idea of forgiveness can be a stumbling block for most people, and it is something I struggle with myself. I know that if I happened to be talking with a group of friends about Rose West, who was complicit in the gruesome torture and murder of several young women, and declared, "It would be right to forgive her," my companions would consider me a madwoman, or at best, a 'bleeding heart liberal'.

Yet someone who, through years of self-searching and anguish, has come to forgive Rose West is Marian Partington, the sister of Lucy, one of the West victims. In her book "If you sit very still", she explains how we have a great need to forgive and to be forgiven. It is an attitude that runs counter to the prevailing way of looking at things. Sadly, most of us, most of the time, are quick to criticise, judge, condemn and, in extreme cases, to cry out for vengeance.

But there is another way, a way that is painful and challenging but eventually life enhancing: the way of forgiveness.

# 91  OTHER WORLDS

I went round to Miriam's for coffee. Her house is like mine, cool in summer, warm in winter. Like me, she has a television and radio, comfortable chairs, paintings on the wall, stacks of books and a fridge full of food.

She handed me a cup of coffee, and with it a photograph of a refugee camp on the Jordan-Syrian border which houses 115,000 Syrian refugees. I gave her an article which I had just been reading about the plight of Bedouin Arabs in Palestine who are so poor they can barely manage to stay alive.

Miriam and I felt sad, angry and powerless. We thought about all the letters we have written about injustice of one sort or another to our Member of Parliament and other politicians. We remembered all the meetings we have attended, all the marches we have walked on, all the prayers we have said.

We sat in heavy silence for a while, till Miriam said, "Do you think it's possible that now, at this minute, two Bedouin women, in their tent, or perhaps two Syrian women in that horrendous camp, are sitting down together, drinking coffee and laughing?"

"God knows" I said, "but I hope so." And we managed, if not a laugh, at least a smile.

## 92  SHARPENING

There is a powerful prayer, the words of a Native American Indian, in which he asks the Great Spirit to "make his ears sharp." As I grow older, I am gradually losing my hearing. Sometimes I have to strain to follow someone's conversation or enjoy the subtleties of a piece of music. My sight is not affected, yet I feel as though I am in some sort of fog, groping my way towards enlightenment.

And when I was reading this prayer I saw that there is a parallel between physical deafness and its spiritual equivalent. Sometimes when I am silent, I try and fail to hear the word of God, and I find myself groping towards some kind of recognition or inspiration.

I realise now that it is unwise to strain and grope my way towards God. And yet it is good to keep my ears sharp, my mind and all my senses alert so that I may be receptive to whatever revelation my God chooses to give me.

## 93   THE LAST ROSE

Every day, this December, I gaze at the last rose of summer which stands in a plain glass on the mantelpiece. None of its petals have fallen, nor have they faded. This rose is exquisite, though dead, and has been for days. Foolishly perhaps, I cannot bring myself to throw it away. It stands very tall, but I see that its stem is far from straight: in two places it bends at an angle. It strikes me that most of us are like this rose; surviving on shaky foundations: part fears, part loss, part weakness. But unlike this once-perfect rose, we try to hide the truth of who we are, the truth of our vulnerability and frailty.

## 94  FOOD

Quite often on a Sunday around lunchtime, we listen to the Food Programme. The presenters talk about exotic foods and healthy foods or there may be a discussion about the relative merits of butter or margarine.

But today the topic was different. The presenter was talking about Food Banks and listening to some of the people who use them. I was particularly struck by one young woman, a single mother. She had a lot to say, though without aggression, about poverty and hunger.

"Some days there's only enough food for one," she said, matter of factly and without self-pity, "so I give it to Jimmy."

I wonder how our country, affluent and theoretically, civilised, a country that is supposedly Christian, has come to this?

And I wonder what I can do about it.

## 95   JUST A MOMENT

This morning we heard on the news about a terrible massacre in a Nairobi shopping centre. Everything about it seemed horrific, until we heard about a four-year-old boy who happened to be there with his mother. When a gunman approached him, pointing his gun at him, he spoke up, and against all the screaming and shouting all around him, the boy said: "You are a very naughty man!" The gunman answered him: "I am not a bad man." and from his pocket he took a Mars bar and gave it to the child, letting him and his mother escape to safety.

After this surprising incident, I wonder what happened next. Did the gunman continue to shoot and kill, or did he run away? Perhaps he was killed himself by the police. And the small boy? Will he grow up to be fearless and wise?

We cannot know the answer to these questions. But surely we can recognise that in the midst of horror, this was a moment of grace.

## 96  NO WORDS

The wind is soughing in the waves of the sapphire sea
and the seagulls are soaring in the summer sky.
We just stand there, looking,
feeling reverence,
saying nothing,
silent.
Sometimes words, however beautiful, are simply:
intrusive.

A friend told me that the Scottish poet George McLeod described the island of Iona as 'a thin place.' where the early Christians were aware of having a 'nearness to the place of angels.' Then, today, barely a week after hearing that, I was listening to the radio when the speaker was describing the seventh century church at Bradwell-on-Sea in Essex. She said it was 'a thin place' where there is only a wisp of tissue between Heaven and Earth.

Thinking about this, I understand that I and many others have experienced what it is like to be in 'a thin place', even if we were hardly aware of it at the time. I have visited many places which are generally accepted to be holy; mostly cathedrals or churches, oases of peace where people have prayed and where I did feel that God was close. But I also remember a tree of very great age and height, and later, a round, still, green, pool that I found quite close to the centre of a busy town. I stood quietly for a while under the tree, and later, by this green pool, and I realise now that both were surely 'thin places' too.

## 98  CLEAN LINEN

I went out into the garden just now and glanced across at my washing which is blowing on the line. I felt a surge of pleasure which surprised me, and perhaps, also a sense of pride.

I am very far from being a good housewife, yet the sight of my clean linen dancing in the bright sunshine and buffeted by a strong west wind makes me rejoice.

Quite often, when I am out in the country, seeing small farmsteads isolated from any other human habitation, I wonder about the farmers' wives. In the early days of my childhood, they would have had no telephones and the only means of transport would have been by horse and cart. Was this a fulfilling life?

Probably most of these women would have had children, and their surroundings were undoubtedly beautiful. They worked hard all the hours of daylight and afterwards in the home. They might have had books but no television and radio. I wonder what made them happy.

Perhaps a line of washing frolicking in the sunshine?

## 99  THE GREAT LONELINESS

I was reading a poem by the American writer Mary Oliver which ended with the words: "The great loneliness". This led me to wonder what she might have meant.

I find myself aching for those I see as experiencing the great loneliness: the widow and the widower, the orphan, the unattractive, those whose home is a prison cell, those who seek refuge in a strange land, the misunderstood, the friendless and the unloved.

When I think of such people I ache, because I guess that most of those who experience the Great Loneliness, suffer in silence, and so, live unconsoled. And I ask myself: is there any value, any use, in such aching? Perhaps only if aching leads to prayer.

## 100 MARY WHOOSH!

This morning I went to church. It was the Feast of the Assumption of Mary into Heaven. The priest told us he had worked in Zambia for some time, where he found it difficult to understand and speak even one of the 67 tribal languages. When it came to this feast day, he had asked for help from a Zambian colleague in translating the word 'assumption'. His friend swooped his arms up into the sky and said 'Whoosh!' After this the people of the parish always celebrated the day as the Feast of Mary Whoosh!

Then this evening, our friend Mary arrived from Teesside, thirty miles away, bringing with her Jacob, Boris, Aleen and John, four young refugees from different African countries where they had suffered torture and tragedy. John is familiar with our town, so Mary suggested he take the others to explore the cliffs, the abbey and the view over the sea.

When they had gone Mary sat back in her chair. She looked completely exhausted.

She is a retired teacher, and for a long number of years she has devoted her life to helping refugees to find justice, to get them safe accommodation, access to health and education. For her it is a full-time occupation and in answer to our questions she told us some of her struggles to help Boris, Jacob, Aleen, John and countless others. As she described the almost daily calls on her to go to court, to the hospital, to woefully inadequate housing, to politicians, to emotionally devastated people, the thought occurred to me: surely this is another Mary Whoosh, transported not up to Heaven, but into the heart of humanity.

# 101 ACCEPTANCE

The other day, my husband, Chris, was cutting the grass when he tripped and fell heavily onto stone, damaging his leg. The kindly neighbours have now forbidden him to cut the grass ever again, but Chris is not happy, because he is a passionate gardener and he thinks he can make a much more beautiful lawn than any one else! What is even worse, when he had to go into hospital for a major operation, he was not so concerned about the heart surgery, but was devastated to be told by the nurses who measured him, that he had lost 5 inches in height! As for me, I saw a photograph last week and for a second, my question was who is that old lady? Then I recognised that it was me.

There comes a time in old age when it's hard to admit that acceptance, rather than achievement, is the thing, and gradually we come to see that this need not be a negative and unfulfilling state in which to find oneself.

There are two ways of looking at acceptance. When an unwished-for fate strikes us we may respond with resignation and give up on life, or we may try to seek some creative response within ourselves. The slaves on American cotton plantations had no choice but to accept their lot - their complete lack of freedom and justice. Yet out of this dreadful situation they gave the world music: spiritual songs and jazz. Tortured and sitting in solitary confinement, the young Russian poet Irina Ratushinskaya, had no choice but to accept her fate, but using scraps of toilet paper she managed to write her inspiring poetry.

And for us, however ordinary and talentless we may feel ourselves to be, however stuck in old age, sickness, loneliness or uselessness, it may sometimes be possible to look up and look out, to find fulfillment. This might be in praying for others, in listening to music, and if we are still blessed with memory, in the enjoyment of the gift of remembering. Rather than slumping in the armchair, or turning over and going back to sleep, we might think of ways to imitate the jazz musicians and improvise!

We buried John today. He did not have a charismatic personality, his death went unrecorded in any national paper or even his local 'rag'. He was an unobtrusive, thoughtful man, intelligent, yes, but also profoundly wise and passionate about the things that mattered to him. His belief: "It's all about love and forgiveness, and being one with the universe.'

I expected to be moved by John's funeral. I knew the poetry and the songs would be inspiring, the tributes poignant. And they were. What I did not expect was to be touched by small things: the dignity of Malcolm, John's six-year-old grandson, as he spoke his prayer so clearly, by the kindness of people who made the 'bunfight' in the church hall after the service so comfortable and pleasant, by the sight of so many people trudging through the mud of the cold, dark wood - it was a green burial - to stand respectfully as the coffin was lowered. Solemn words were spoken, gold finches sang, people wept, and two-year-old

Emily danced at the edge of her grandfather's grave, happy, oblivious, but still, as John would have said, part of it all.

## 104  SUMMER DAYS 2014

On the beach, sunshine and blue skies,
children are playing,
little boys running and leaping.
little girls skipping and dancing,
everyone laughing
or shrieking with delight
at the splash of the waves on bare feet.

Then, in the space of a few seconds,
the sky darkens.
There is a moment of shocked silence,
silence broken by the sound of terror:
the bombs fall, the children fall,
and in this awful silence
the beach is strewn with the bodies
of Gaza's children:
twisted, mangled, bloodied,
and all of them,
dead.

## 105  GROWN-OVER

Earlier in this book, I wrote about my excitement and wonder as a small child when I first saw the snow, and how my mother could not restrain me from rushing out to experience it. And more recently, I saw a little boy catch his first sight of the expanse of sandy beach and the sparkling sea beyond. He gave a cry of delight, then ran as fast as his short legs would carry him, until he reached the sparkling waves.

I wonder if many, if not most of us, have lost that wonder and excitement as we grow older, and so perhaps it would be good if, now and again, we could free ourselves from the grown-up, grown-over clutter of our lives. Then we could give time to lift up our faces to the falling rain, to be still and let the beauty of silence wash over us. We could look long at the waves in the sea, the rainbows in puddles, the clouds in the sky, and put ourselves in touch again with our universe and our God.

There is an old song I like very much. I think it's intended for children, and it begins:

*"Would you like to swing on a star,*
*carry moonbeams home in a jar?"*

Now, I am all for ambition, achievement and passion, for climbing the highest mountains, diving into the deepest oceans, travelling the world, working in refugee camps or hospices, saving the planet or fighting for justice..... I think it can only be good to live life to the full. But there comes a time when the focus switches, when achievement gives way to acceptance, when, unless our minds are fractured or we are suffering great pain, we can become enriched and fulfilled by a willingness to surrender to whatever is to come, and above all, by a growing realisation that the Kingdom of God is very near, indeed, sometimes, within us. Then we find happiness in stillness, in the richness of memory, in simple beauty and the joy of friendship.

All this I believe to be true, and yet I confess that sometimes, even now, I have a sneaking longing to swing on a star!

## 107  STATISTIC

In the land where Christ was born,
a young farmer, father of four, was
tending his olive trees,
when a bomb exploded and wounded him.
There was only the screaming pain,
and then the sweet realisation
that he was no longer responsible
for anything, any more.
And so, he died.
The statistician said, "That's a thousand
million innocent civilians
killed in war. Then he checked his
computer, and said,
"Oh, no, I'm sorry. That was a mistake.
It is a thousand million innocent civilians
and one."
At least **he** was sorry -
(about the incorrect statistic).

## 108  IBRAHIM

When I heard the shot, somehow I knew
it was Ali,
and that he was dead. And in that moment I saw
that all the colour was leached from my world.
I went into the house and sat down on the floor.
I rocked myself and wept, but I did not wail.
I could not bear, just then,
the other women, the other young widows,
running to me and crowding me
with their wailing and comforting.
Then someone entered. My young son ran to me,
his tears flowing fast. He pulled me to my feet.
"Mother," he said, "I will see to the trees,
I will fetch the water, every day."
He was six years old.
I looked at him: at the firm set of his mouth,
and the fierce brightness in his eyes. I said
"Ibrahim, you are the image of your father."

One warm summer evening, Jacuba and Aime trudged across the big field, thankful to be miles away from the city and their dismal housing.

Just as the rosy colour was fading from the sky, they stopped at a corner and lay down on the grass. They stayed there quite still for a long time, gazing upwards, watching as the sky slowly darkened.

At first one by one, then gradually, tens, hundreds, thousands of stars were filling every space above them.

"It's just like home!" Aime whispered, although no-one could hear them.

Jacuba, older and wiser, said, "No, Aime, don't think of Guinea. Take courage. True, the stars are shining brightly, but now we must accept that Britain is our home."

## 110   THE PINK PEOPLE

I like the pink people; I like them a lot. I don't mean the ones you see walking in the streets; I mean the ones at a place where we go on a bus. It's a long way, but it's lovely when we get there.

The pink people look so happy to see us. They have big smiles and they have balloons and toys for us and there's lots of wonderful food. This time after the feast, a nice pink lady took me and my friends to paddle in the sea. It was such fun! A pink man took my brothers on a boat, right into the sea. My mother talked to the ladies and they filled a big bag with more food and toys and clothes.

When we got home, even my mother, who cries a lot, was smiling.

I said "Mother, I think you like the pink people too."

She said "Oh, Precious, you are a silly little girl! These people are not pink, they are white."

But I have looked and looked at their faces and I know they are pink.

# 111 TRANQUILLITY

Quite unexpectedly, someone gave me an extravagant bouquet of gorgeous flowers. I was surprised, and touched, and of course I was pleased and grateful. Flower-arranging is definitely not one of my talents, so someone else placed them in a big jug and put them where I can see them from my chair.

There are a lot of flowers of different kinds and shapes. The colours give an over-all impression of richness: dark red, a softer red, and pink, purple, a softer purple and mauve.

But from where I sit there is one flower that stands out from all the rest. Centre front in the lush arrangement, is a single white carnation, and it draws my eye continually. It seems to symbolise purity, purity and yes, a kind of holiness. Looking at it brings me a sense of tranquillity.

## 112   THE CALL

The missionary
was called to heathen lands.
He travelled in fear and danger
seeking souls for Christ.

The aid worker
was called to hellish countries.
She travelled in fear and danger
healing the sick and comforting the dying.

But I was deaf, I heard no call.
I said a few prayers
and sent a bit of money,
and was comfortable.

## 113  GOD

Beyond the tumult
and the suffering
beyond materialism
and indifference,
Somewhere, somehow, sometime
there will be peace,
and love, too,
because there is hope,
and there is God.

## 114 JESUS

Jesus, I long for you;
I need you in my life.
I long for your truth,
your forgiveness and your love.

And I know that you, too,
are filled with longing:
longing for me, and for all, God's children,
that we may be one,
and the Kingdom may come.